THE
TOTALLY
TOMATO
COOKBOOK

The
TOTALLY
TOMATO
COOKBOOK

By Helene Siegel

*Illustrated by
Carolyn Vibbert*

CELESTIAL ARTS
BERKELEY, CALIFORNIA

With special thanks to Ophelia Chong
for sharing her bounty.

Celestial Arts Publishing
P.O. Box 7123
Berkeley, CA 94707
Printed in Singapore

The Totally Tomato Cookbook is produced by becker&mayer!, Ltd.

Cover design and illustration: Bob Greisen
Interior design and typesetting: Susan Hernday
Interior illustrations: Carolyn Vibbert

Library of Congress Cataloging-in-Publication Data:
Siegel, Helene.
   Totally Tomato Cookbook/ by Helene Siegel.
      p.   cm.
   ISBN 0-89087-788-2
   1. Cookery (Tomato)   2. Tomato   I. Title.
   TX803. T6S54   1996
   641.6'5642—dc20   95-45226
                                                    CIP

Other cookbooks in this series:
The Totally Eggplant Cookbook
The Totally Picnic Cookbook
The Totally Pizza Cookbook

CONTENTS

6
INTRODUCTION

9
BRIGHT SOUPS AND STARTERS

22
THE RED STANDARD FOR SAUCES AND SALSAS

36
JUICY SALADS AND SANDWICHES

50
TOMATO CENTERPIECES

68
TOMATOEY SIDES

77
TOMATO SCRAPS

90
SWEET SURPRISES AND MORE

96
CONVERSIONS

INTRODUCTION

The history of the tomato is mired in controversy. From the beginning people have wondered: Is it a fruit or a vegetable? Poison or miracle cure? Easy to grow or voracious weed? Deliciously natural fruit of the vine, or symbol of our high-tech future?

As a major tomato cook (I was once reprimanded by an editor for using too many), even I have to agree with Ralph Waldo Emerson that the taste for tomatoes, eaten straight, is an acquired one. My first bite was taken on a dare as a young child and I was not immediately impressed.

Once I started cooking, however, my feelings grew.

Unlike any other fruit (or vegetable) except perhaps garlic and onions, tomatoes act as a seasoning. Chopped and added to soups, stews, and sauces, they lift the other flavors with their uncommon blend of acidity and sweetness, and make them sing just a little bit clearer and higher. Eaten fresh off the vine, dressed simply with some good olive oil, salt, pepper, and herbs, they are incomparable; puréed into a soup they are heaven to look at and to taste.

So whether you grow your own, buy them at the market, or receive them as a gift from a friend with a bountiful garden, seek out some delicious, fresh tomatoes next summer. Then dig in and enjoy!

BRIGHT SOUPS AND STARTERS

COLD TOMATO
AND CUCUMBER SOUP

This elegant gazpacho is a personal summer favorite. Serve at parties, garnished with croutons or slices of toasted baguette.

2 tablespoons olive oil
2 garlic cloves, chopped
2½ pounds tomatoes, peeled, seeded, and
    chopped
salt and freshly ground pepper
2 large cucumbers, peeled, seeded, and
    chopped
½ cup tomato juice
1½ tablespoons red wine vinegar
3 dashes Tabasco
thinly sliced chives for garnish

Heat the oil in a medium skillet over medium heat. Cook the garlic briefly to release its aroma, then add tomatoes, salt, and pepper. Cook at a medium boil, stirring occasionally, for 5 minutes. Remove from heat.

Place the cucumbers in a food processor or blender and purée. Add the tomatoes and remaining ingredients. Purée until smooth, adding more tomato juice to taste. Chill and serve ice cold, garnished with chives.

SERVES 4

TOMATO FENNEL BISQUE

To set the tone for an elegant dinner party, try starting with this refined French classic inspired by chefs Mary Sue Milliken and Susan Feniger.

2 tablespoons butter
2 leeks, white parts, thinly sliced
1 large fennel bulb, stalks separated and
    thinly sliced
3 large tomatoes, seeded and chopped
3 cups chicken *or* vegetable stock
salt and freshly ground pepper to taste
½ cup heavy cream
1 tablespoon Pernod *or* other anise
    flavored liqueur
3 dashes Tabasco
fennel leaves for garnish

Melt butter in heavy stockpot over medium heat. Cook leeks and fennel until soft, about 15 minutes. Add tomatoes, stock, salt, and pepper. Bring to boil, reduce to simmer, and cook about 20 minutes.

Transfer to food processor or blender in batches and purée until smooth. Strain back into pot and pour in cream. Bring back to boil, stir in Pernod and Tabasco. Remove from heat. Serve hot, garnished with wispy fennel leaves.

SERVES 6

ROASTED TOMATO, CORN, AND TORTILLA SOUP

3 large tomatoes
1 small onion, unpeeled
3 garlic cloves, unpeeled
1 jalapeño pepper with seeds, stemmed
1/2 cup vegetable oil
1/2 teaspoon ground cumin
1 quart chicken stock
salt to taste
2 ears fresh corn, kernels removed from cobs
8 dry corn tortillas, halved, and cut in strips
cilantro leaves, lime wedges, and shredded
    mozzarella cheese for garnish

Preheat the broiler and line baking sheet with foil. Place tomatoes, onion, garlic, and jalapeño on sheet. Broil, turning frequently, until charred all over, about 20 minutes. Peel onion and garlic and quarter onion. Transfer everything to a food processor and purée until smooth.

Heat 1 tablespoon of the oil in large stockpot over high heat. Sauté cumin briefly. Pour in puréed mixture and cook about 5 minutes. Add chicken stock and salt. Bring back to boil, reduce to simmer, and cook—skimming and discarding foam as necessary—about 20 minutes. Stir in corn kernels and cook 1 minute longer.

Fry tortilla strips in remaining oil in small skillet. Drain on paper towels. Serve hot soup garnished with tortilla strips, cilantro, lime wedges, and cheese.

SERVES 4

TOMATOES WITH CRAB AND CORN SALAD

A light, no-fuss, stuffed tomato to brighten the senses.

6 medium tomatoes, halved
1 tablespoon olive oil
1 cup fresh corn kernels
1 garlic clove, minced
$\frac{1}{2}$ pound flaked, cleaned crabmeat
1 celery rib, diced
juice of $\frac{1}{2}$ lemon
3 tablespoons mayonnaise
Tabasco and freshly ground pepper

With a teaspoon, scrape out and discard tomato pulp and seeds. Place halves, cut-side down, on paper towels to drain.

Heat oil in small skillet over high heat. Sauté corn and garlic about 1 minute.

Combine crabmeat, celery, and corn in mixing bowl. Sprinkle with lemon juice, add mayonnaise, and gently stir to combine. Season to taste with Tabasco and pepper. Fill each tomato half with a generous tablespoonful of crab salad. Serve cold.

SERVES 6 TO 12

Choosing the Best
Let your nose, and the calendar, be your guide when choosing tomatoes. Color is not a reliable indicator. Late summer produces the best, most sugary tomatoes. Look for smooth, unwrinkled skin without mold. Don't be too concerned about cracking at the stem end; it could mean vine-ripening. Store tomatoes at room temperature, since cold deadens their taste. The flavor of tomatoes dissipates quickly—20 minutes after cutting or chopping.

TOMATO MANGO CEVICHE

Mango and tomato add a jolt of tropical flavor and color to this traditional South American fish salad.

½ pound red snapper fillet, trimmed
¾ cup lime juice
1 cup diced red onion
2 medium tomatoes, seeded and diced
2 tablespoons olive oil
1 tablespoon red wine vinegar
1 jalapeño chile, seeded and diced
1 mango, peeled and diced
2 tablespoons fresh chopped cilantro
salt, pepper, and Tabasco

Cut fish into ½-inch cubes. Place in shallow glass or ceramic bowl, pour on lime juice, cover with plastic wrap, and chill 4 to 5 hours, or until the largest piece is opaque in center. Drain fish, discarding the juice.

Combine remaining ingredients in bowl, add fish, and toss to combine. Adjust seasonings and serve or store in the refrigerator up to 24 hours.

SERVES 4

How to Peel and Seed

Many classic European recipes call for removing the skins and seeds of tomatoes, since they are considered less digestible. To peel your tomatoes, first bring a pot of water to a boil. Lightly score an X on the bottom ends and trim the stems. Plunge in simmering water for 20 seconds, remove, and rinse with cold water to stop cooking. Peel with a paring knife, cut in half crosswise, and gently squeeze or scoop out seeds with a small spoon.

TOMATO ONION TARTS

Individual puff pastries topped with sweet tomato slices make an elegant first course for a special dinner party.

½ pound (1 sheet) frozen puff pastry
2 tablespoons olive oil
1 large onion, thinly sliced
½ teaspoon chopped fresh thyme
2 large tomatoes, cut into ¼-inch slices
8 Kalamata *or* Niçoise olives

Defrost puff pastry according to directions and roll out to a 10-inch square on floured board. Neatly cut into 8 small squares and place on uncoated baking sheet. Pierce all over with fork and chill.

Meanwhile preheat oven to 400 degrees F.

Heat oil in skillet over moderate heat. Cook onion with thyme, stirring occasionally, until soft and beginning to brown, about 20 minutes. Transfer to small bowl and chill 15 minutes.

When onions cool, divide and spread on each pastry square, leaving rim bare. Top each with a tomato slice or two and an olive. Bake about 30 minutes, until edges are puffed and golden. Cool slightly and serve.

SERVES 8

THE RED STANDARD
FOR
SAUCES AND SALSAS

SALSA FRESCA

This is the basic red salsa for chips, tacos, or anything else that needs jazzing up.

3 large tomatoes, chopped
$\frac{1}{2}$ red onion, diced
2 serrano or jalapeño chiles, stemmed and
    finely diced with seeds
$\frac{1}{2}$ cup chopped fresh cilantro
2 tablespoons lime juice
$\frac{1}{4}$ teaspoon salt
Tabasco to taste (optional)

Combine ingredients in mixing bowl. Toss well and taste for seasonings. Adjust with salt and Tabasco. Store in the refrigerator, in sealed container, as long as 1 day.

MAKES $4\frac{1}{2}$ CUPS

FRESH TOMATO SAUCE FOR PASTA

Use the freshest, sweetest, most sun-ripened toma-toes when making such an unadorned sauce.

2½ pounds tomatoes
4 tablespoons butter
1 cup diced onion
1 garlic clove, minced
coarse salt and freshly ground pepper
¼ cup chopped fresh basil *or* Italian parsley

Cut tomatoes in half and squeeze out seeds. Place in food processor and roughly chop.

Melt 3 tablespoons of the butter in a large saucepan over moderate heat. Cook onion and garlic until soft, about 7 minutes. Add tomatoes, salt, and pepper, and simmer uncovered, until thickened, 20 to 30 minutes. Stir in remaining butter and basil or parsley, and remove from heat.

MAKES 3 CUPS, ENOUGH FOR 1 POUND PASTA

ROASTED TOMATO SALSA

Roasted salsa has a deeper, more burnished flavor than fresh salsa. It goes naturally with foods from the grill.

6 medium tomatoes
4 garlic cloves, unpeeled
1 small white onion, unpeeled
1 jalapeño chile, stemmed
1 tablespoon vegetable oil
1/2 teaspoon salt

Preheat broiler and line baking sheet with a sheet of foil.

Arrange tomatoes, garlic, onion, and jalapeño on sheet, and broil, turning frequently, until evenly charred, 15 to 20 minutes. Let cool.

When cool enough to handle, remove garlic and onion skins, and transfer all, including juices on tray, to blender or food processor fitted with blade. Pulse until a chunky purée is formed.

Heat vegetable oil in medium saucepan over high heat. Pour in tomato mixture, season with salt, and simmer about 5 minutes. Serve hot or cold with grilled meat, chicken, or fish. This salsa is also delicious with eggs and chips.

MAKES 3 CUPS

ALLA CHECCA

This classic raw tomato sauce makes summer cooking a breeze at least one night a week—truly a boon for the summer gardener and cook.

5 tomatoes, cored and diced
4 garlic cloves, minced
1/2 cup chopped fresh basil
1/2 cup extra virgin olive oil
salt
grated Parmesan cheese

Combine tomatoes, garlic, basil, and olive oil in medium bowl. Add salt to taste, cover with plastic wrap, and let sit on counter at least 2 or as long as 10 hours. Pour over hot pasta and add grated Parmesan to taste.

MAKES ENOUGH FOR 1 POUND PASTA

Tomatoes in the Garden

According to the National Garden Association, tomatoes are the most popular garden vegetable in the U.S. More than 27 million Americans grow their own tomatoes—some with better luck than others. The plants thrive in a hot, dry climate and need more moisture when they are taking root than when they flower. Do not prune back leaves. Use a wire cage to encourage growth, and water from beneath once the plants flower and fruit. Leafier plants, as a rule, produce sweeter fruit. In Southern California some popular varieties are the early blooming EARLY GIRL, midsummer CHAMPION, SWEET 100 CHERRY, and disease-resistant HUSKY.

INSTANT ARRABBIATA SAUCE

I couldn't omit this recipe for the quickest, tastiest sauce out of a can.

> 2 tablespoons olive oil
> 4 garlic cloves, minced
> 1 teaspoon red chile flakes
> 1 (28-ounce) can Italian crushed tomatoes
> salt
> 1 tablespoon dried crumbled oregano

Heat the olive oil in a large skillet over medium-low heat. Cook garlic and red pepper flakes, swirling frequently, until garlic is soft but not brown. Add tomatoes, salt, and oregano. Bring to boil, reduce to a simmer, and cook, uncovered until thickened, about 20 minutes. Season to taste with salt and additional pepper if desired. Toss with hot pasta.

MAKES ENOUGH FOR 1 POUND PASTA

Tomatoes and the American Way
The popularity of the tomato in America is closely tied to the growth of the commercial canning industry. The Campbell's factory, which opened in 1869, needed a large commercial crop to process its soup. Although tomatoes were grown in Thomas Jefferson's garden, and instructions for preserving tomatoes can be found in one colonial cookbook, creative tomato cookery didn't really blossom until the late 19th and early 20th centuries.

TOMATO AND ARTICHOKE PASTA SALAD

This strongly flavored, fresh sauce combines two distinctive Mediterranean tastes.

6 plum tomatoes, seeded and julienned
1 cup julienned marinated artichoke hearts
3 garlic cloves, minced
2 teaspoons chopped fresh basil
salt and freshly ground pepper
$\frac{1}{2}$ to $\frac{3}{4}$ cup olive oil
1 pound penne *or* short tube pasta, cooked
    and drained

Combine all of the ingredients except pasta in medium bowl. Stir well, cover with plastic wrap, and marinate at room temperature at least 1 or as long as 8 hours.

Pour over hot pasta and mix, or serve with cold pasta as a salad.

SERVES 6

The Italian Way

Italians, like most Europeans, gazed with suspicion on that exotic fruit that went on to become the pomodoro, *or "golden apple." Although it appeared as early as 1692 in a Sicilian cookbook, it wasn't embraced by most cooks until the last century. Europeans used the tomato as an ornamental in the garden, an aphrodisiac in the bedroom, and an herbal remedy long before they cooked with it.*

TOMATO COULIS

Coulis *is the French term for a smooth puréed vegetable or fruit sauce. This one is excellent on a fine pasta such as spaghettini, rice, or with a platter of steamed vegetables. Leftover sauce may be frozen.*

3 tablespoons butter
1 medium onion, sliced
2 carrots, thinly sliced
2¼ pounds tomatoes, peeled and chopped
3 sprigs thyme
salt and freshly ground pepper
¼ teaspoon sugar (optional)
2 teaspoons dry sherry

Heat 2 tablespoons of the butter in a large saucepan over moderate heat. Sauté onion and carrots until softened. Add tomatoes, thyme, salt, pepper, and sugar, if desired, and cook, uncovered, over medium-high heat 15 minutes. Remove and discard thyme sprigs.

Transfer to food processor and purée until smooth. Return to pan and warm over low heat. Stir in remaining tablespoon butter and sherry, until butter is melted. Remove from heat.

MAKES 1 QUART, ENOUGH FOR 2 POUNDS PASTA

JUICY SALADS AND SANDWICHES

TOMATO AND MOZZARELLA SALAD

This classic Italian dish, known as caprese, *deserves a beautiful platter and the very best, ripe tomatoes.*

2 large tomatoes, cut in ¼-inch slices
8 ounces fresh mozzarella, cut in ¼-inch slices
10 basil leaves
salt and freshly ground pepper
extra virgin olive oil

Tile tomatoes, mozzarella, and basil on serving platter. Extra pieces can be stacked attractively. Season with salt and pepper and lightly drizzle with oil. Serve immediately or chill.

SERVES 4 TO 6

CHOPPED GREEK SALAD

When the temperature is rising, what could be more refreshing than cool cukes and sharp feta?

4 medium tomatoes, seeded and chopped
1 large cucumber, peeled, seeded, and
    diced
4 scallions, both white and light green
    parts, sliced
1/2 cup chopped fresh Italian parsley *or*
    oregano
1/2 cup crumbled feta cheese
1/4 cup red wine vinegar
1/4 cup plus 2 tablespoons olive oil
3 to 4 dashes Tabasco
salt and freshly ground pepper

Combine tomatoes, cucumber, scallions, parsley or oregano, and feta cheese in mixing bowl.

In small bowl, whisk together vinegar, oil, Tabasco, salt, and pepper. Pour over salad, toss well, and chill or serve.

SERVES 4

How to Julienne a Tomato

Thin strips of meaty plum or Roma tomatoes are elegant additions to salads. First cut tomato into quarters, lengthwise. Then trim out and discard the seeds. Cut remaining pulp in strips lengthwise.

CUBAN SALAD

Tomatoes and avocados are a popular combination in many Latin American countries.

2 large tomatoes, cut in thin wedges
1 Haas avocado, peeled, halved, and thinly
  sliced
1/2 large red onion, thinly sliced
salt and freshly ground pepper
juice of 1/2 lime
3 tablespoons olive oil

Place tomato wedges in shallow serving bowl or platter. Top with avocado slices and sprinkle with onion. Season generously with pepper and salt. Drizzle with lime juice and olive oil and serve. (Do not toss.)

SERVES 2 TO 4

Tomato Types

The original tomato was a small, yellow-orange fruit with heavily ribbed sections. The most popular modern tomato is EARLY GIRL, known for its superior blend of sweetness and acidity. Small, round, red cherry tomatoes and long, thin, red plums, or Roma tomatoes, are excellent for sauces as they have fewer seeds and less water. Look for big, juicy "beefsteaks," at farmers markets during summer. They are superior for slicing into sandwiches or salads. Green tomatoes are unripe red ones, and tomatillos, sometimes incorrectly referred to as green tomatoes, are a totally different species.

TOMATO WHITE BEAN SALAD

This tasty little salad is so creamy and luscious, it's hard to believe it is healthful as well. Serve with roasted fish as a side dish or salsa.

4 garlic cloves, peeled
2 tablespoons oil-packed
   sun-dried tomatoes
5 tablespoons olive oil
3 tablespoons lemon juice
salt and freshly ground pepper
2 (15-ounce) cans white beans, rinsed
2 plum tomatoes, chopped
1 to 2 jalapeño chiles, seeded and diced
1 tablespoon chopped fresh Italian parsley

Bring a small saucepan of water to boil. Blanch garlic for 5 minutes and remove with slotted spoon. Transfer to blender or food processor. Add sun-dried tomatoes, olive oil, lemon juice, salt, and pepper. Purée until smooth.

Combine beans, tomatoes, chiles, and parsley in mixing bowl. Pour on dressing, mix well and serve or chill.

SERVES 4

SPINACH BACON SALAD
WITH TOMATO VINAIGRETTE

*For those who like their tomato salads juicy,
acidic, and fairly dripping with vitamin C.*

1/2 pound bacon, cut in 1/2-inch lengths
2 bunches spinach leaves, washed, dried,
   and torn
12 cherry tomatoes, halved

TOMATO VINAIGRETTE
2 medium tomatoes, peeled, seeded, and
   diced
1 tablespoon chopped, oil-packed,
   sun-dried tomatoes
3 tablespoons lemon juice
1 shallot, chopped
1 1/2 teaspoons minced garlic
1/3 cup olive oil
salt and freshly ground pepper

Fry bacon over low heat, turning frequently, and drain on paper towels.

Toss spinach leaves and tomatoes together in salad bowl and chill.

Combine diced tomatoes, sun-dried tomatoes, lemon juice, shallot, and garlic in blender and purée. With machine on, drizzle in olive oil. Season to taste with salt and pepper. Pour enough dressing over cold salad to coat leaves. Toss well and sprinkle top with bacon bits. (Leftover vinaigrette may be stored in the refrigerator up to 5 days.)

SERVES 4 TO 6

COUNTRY TOMATO PESTO SANDWICH

I am a fan of rustic vegetable sandwiches such as this one—ideal for trips to the beach.

2 thick slices country bread
pesto
thickly sliced medium tomatoes
thinly sliced onion
salt and freshly ground pepper

Generously spread 1 side each of 2 bread slices with pesto. Top 1 with a single layer of tomato and onion and close with second slice, pesto-side down. Serve at room temperature.

MAKES 1

Tomato Roots

The original tomato plant was a native of Peru, Ecuador, Bolivia, and Chile. Unlike beans and corn, it was not sown as a crop by the Indians. It was among the new foods brought back to Europe by Cortez and gradually disseminated through Spain to Portugal, Africa, then back to North America. By some fluke of culinary immigration, the tomato did not appear in Chinese cuisine until about twenty years ago. It has made vast inroads since then.

GRILLED MOZZARELLA, EGGPLANT, AND TOMATO PANINI

1 medium eggplant, stemmed, peeled, and
    cut crosswise into ½-inch slices
olive oil for coating
salt
2 individual baguettes or long crusty rolls
½ cup olive oil
4 teaspoons herbes de Provence (a mix of
    thyme, rosemary, bay, basil, and savory)
½ teaspoon minced garlic
½ teaspoon salt
freshly ground pepper
6 ounces mozzarella, thinly sliced
1 large tomato, thickly sliced crosswise

Preheat oven to 450 degrees F. Arrange eggplant in single layer on a baking sheet coated with olive oil. Drizzle with oil, season with salt, and roast until golden, about 5 minutes per side. Turn on broiler.

Split rolls open and place, cut-side up, on baking sheet. In small bowl, whisk together olive oil, herbs, garlic, salt, and pepper. Brush tops of bread and broil less than 1 minute to crisp. Remove. Top 2 halves with cheese and 2 with eggplant slices. Return to broiler just to melt cheese.

Top eggplant with layer of tomato slices, brush with remaining oil, cover with melted cheese half, and slice to serve.

MAKES 2 SERVINGS

TOMATO
CENTERPIECES

POACHED SALMON IN TOMATO AND BASIL BROTH

Juices from the salmon combine with fresh tomatoes and basil in this easy but elegant one-skillet supper.

4 medium tomatoes, peeled, seeded, and puréed
$1/4$ cup dry white wine
2 tablespoons butter, cut in thin slices
4 (4-ounce) salmon fillets
1 bunch basil leaves
salt and freshly ground pepper to taste

Combine tomatoes, wine, and butter in large skillet. Place fillets on top and turn heat to high. Top with basil, salt, and pepper. Cover tightly, reduce heat to low, and simmer 10 minutes. Serve fish with sauce over rice or pasta.

SERVES 4

TOMATO CHEESE PIE

With frozen pie crusts available in the super market freezer, a cozy tomato cheese pie need only be minutes away.

2 frozen (9-inch) pie crusts
2 pounds small or medium tomatoes,
    peeled, seeded, and cut in thin wedges
2 garlic cloves, minced
salt and freshly ground pepper
1 1/2 cups grated cheddar cheese
1/4 cup heavy cream

Preheat oven to 400 degrees F. Defrost pie crusts according to directions.

Fill bottom crust with tomatoes. Sprinkle with garlic, salt, and pepper. Scatter cheese over top. Drizzle on cream. Cover with top crust, crimping edges to seal. Trim and discard excess dough. Cut 4 (1-inch) slits in top crust. Place on baking sheet and chill 30 minutes.

Brush top with extra cream to glaze and bake until nicely browned, about 40 minutes. Cool on rack and serve hot or room temperature.

SERVES 6 TO 8

The Plant

Tomatoes are classified by botanists as a fruit. They are a member of the nightshade family, and as such their leaves are toxic. Legally, tomatoes have been considered a vegetable since the U.S. Supreme Court ruled in 1893 to apply vegetable tariffs to them.

SEARED BEEF WITH FRESH TOMATOES AND ARUGULA

This elegant entrée was inspired by chef Celestino Drago of Los Angeles.

1 pound beef tenderloin
salt and freshly ground pepper
2 tablespoons olive oil
2 tablespoons water
1 bunch fresh arugula, chopped
5 garlic cloves, minced
3 plum tomatoes, seeded and julienned

Cut the beef against the grain into $1/4$-inch slices. Pound to flatten, and season all over with salt and pepper.

Heat oil and water in large skillet over medium-high heat. Cook the basil, garlic, and tomato 2 to 3 minutes to wilt. Add beef in 2 batches, pushing finished pieces to the side of the pan, and cook 1 minute per side. Season to taste with salt and pepper and serve hot.

SERVES 4

PAN-FRIED SHARK WITH TOMATOES AND LEMON

You may substitute other fleshy whitefish such as mahimahi or bluefish if shark is not available.

4 (5-ounce) shark fillets
salt and freshly ground pepper
2 tablespoons olive oil
¼ cup chopped fresh Italian parsley
1 large tomato, roughly chopped
juice of ½ lemon

Season fish all over with salt and pepper.

Heat the oil in a large nonstick skillet over high heat. Sear fish 1 minute each side. Reduce heat to moderate and cook an additional 2 minutes per side. Then reduce heat to low, add parsley, tomato, and lemon juice, and cover pan. Cook until fish is opaque in center, about 4 minutes longer. Place fish on individual plates and spoon on sauce to serve.

SERVES 4

STEAMED MUSSELS WITH GARLIC, TOMATOES, AND SAFFRON

¼ cup olive oil
6 garlic cloves, minced
2 medium tomatoes, seeded and diced
½ cup chopped fresh Italian parsley
1½ cups dry white wine
¼ teaspoon saffron threads, chopped
¼ teaspoon dried red chile flakes
50 mussels, cleaned and bearded
salt and freshly ground pepper

Heat olive oil in large stockpot over moderate heat. Sauté garlic, tomatoes, and parsley until fragrant, about 5 minutes. Add wine, saffron, and red chile flakes. Bring to a boil and cook 5 minutes.

Add the mussels, reduce heat to medium, and cover the pot. Cook, shaking occasionally, 8 to 10 minutes, until mussels open. Remove and discard closed shells, adjust broth with salt and pepper, and ladle into bowls to serve.

SERVES 4

The Health Connection
Tomatoes are 95 percent water, 5 percent sugar, and brimming with vitamins A and C. They contain a carotene that is thought to inhibit cancer, and they are the best source of nutrients of all the fruits and vegetables in the American diet. Not bad for a fruit that began life as a poison.

MEDITERRANEAN SEA SCALLOPS

If a trip to the Riviera is not in the budget right now, try this elegant dish instead.

4 large tomatoes, peeled, seeded, and
    chopped
1 1/2 tablespoons Pernod *or* anise liqueur
salt and freshly ground pepper
1 pound sea scallops, halved across width
2 tablespoons olive oil
1 tablespoon butter
1/2 cup chopped fresh basil

Purée tomatoes in blender. Combine in bowl with Pernod, salt, and pepper. Reserve.

Season scallops with salt and pepper. Heat oil in large skillet over high heat. Sauté scallops until opaque, about 1 minute per side. With slotted spoon, transfer to platter.

Add reserved tomatoes to pan. Bring to a boil and cook over high heat until reduced by one third. Turn heat to low, stir in scallops, butter, and basil. Cook until butter just melts, about 1 minute. Season to taste with salt and pepper. Serve over bed of rice or pasta.

SERVES 4 TO 6

EGGS RANCHEROS

This traditional Mexican egg dish makes a nice simple supper for two.

  vegetable oil for frying
  4 corn tortillas
  4 eggs
  1 cup "Roasted Tomato Salsa" (page 26),
      warmed
  2 tablespoons crumbled feta cheese
  2 tablespoons fresh cilantro leaves
  freshly ground pepper

Pour oil into small skillet to depth of $\frac{1}{4}$ inch. Heat over moderate flame and fry tortillas, 1 at a time, until barely crisp, about 1 minute. Drain on paper towels.

Spoon 1 tablespoon of oil from small pan into large nonstick skillet. Fry eggs, all at once, sunny-side up, until whites are just set.

To serve, place 2 tortillas on each plate, slightly overlapping, and top each with an egg. Spoon the warm sauce over whites and tortillas, leaving the yolks uncovered. Sprinkle cheese over all and garnish with cilantro. Sprinkle pepper over yolks and serve.

SERVES 2

STUFFED TOMATOES WITH SPRING VEGETABLES

Here is an easy, low fat, vegetarian entrée, full of flavor and beautiful color.

8 large firm tomatoes
2 tablespoons olive oil
2 shallots, chopped
1 garlic clove, minced
8 mushrooms, chopped
1 ear corn, kernels removed
1/2 cup (1/4-inch lengths) thin asparagus
1/2 cup tomato purée
salt and freshly ground pepper
1/2 teaspoon ground cumin
1 cup cooked rice
1/4 cup Kalamata olives, chopped
1/4 cup chopped fresh basil

Preheat oven to 350 degrees F. Slice ¼ inch off top of each tomato and reserve. Scoop out centers, and drain shells on paper towels, cut-side down.

Heat olive oil in medium skillet over high heat. Sauté shallots, garlic, and mushrooms 1 minute. Add corn and asparagus and cook another minute. Add tomato purée, salt, pepper, and cumin, and cook over moderate heat until nearly dry. Stir in rice, olives, and basil, and remove from heat. Cool.

Sprinkle tomato interiors with salt and pepper, and place on olive oil-coated baking sheet. Stuff each with rice mixture and cover with reserved tops. Bake 20 minutes to soften. Cool slightly and serve.

SERVES 4 TO 8

TURKEY WITH TOMATOES AND CHILES

Serve this healthful dish with warm tortillas or rice for a well-balanced family meal.

1 pound thinly sliced turkey cutlets
salt, pepper, and paprika to taste
3 tablespoons olive oil
3 garlic cloves, sliced
1 onion, thinly sliced
3 plum tomatoes, cut in eighths lengthwise
1 red bell pepper, roasted, seeded, and sliced
1 Anaheim chile, roasted, seeded, and sliced
juice of 2 oranges

Season turkey all over with salt, pepper, and paprika. Heat 2 tablespoons of oil in large nonstick skillet over high heat. Sauté turkey until white, about 1 minute on each side. Reserve on platter.

Add remaining tablespoon of oil to pan and reduce heat to medium. Cook garlic and onion until softened and beginning to caramelize. Add tomatoes, red pepper, chile, salt, pepper, and paprika to taste. Cook at medium-high for 5 minutes. Pour in orange juice, cook 1 minute longer, and return turkey to pan. Cook, turning turkey once or twice, just to heat through, about 1 minute. Serve hot.

SERVES 4

TOMATOEY SIDES

STIR-FRIED CHERRY TOMATOES

The inspiration for this sparkling stir-fry came from French chef Roger Vergé. Serve over angel hair pasta for a complete meal.

1½ tablespoons olive oil
2 cups cherry tomatoes, stemmed, washed, and dried
3 garlic cloves, minced
2 tablespoons fresh chopped tarragon, thyme, *or* basil
salt and freshly ground pepper
2 teaspoons balsamic vinegar

Heat olive oil in large skillet over high heat. Sauté tomatoes about 1 minute. Add garlic, herbs, salt, pepper, and vinegar, and briefly stir-fry. Serve hot.

SERVES 4

TOMATO ZUCCHINI GRATIN

- ¼ cup olive oil
- 4 medium tomatoes, stemmed and thinly sliced
- 4 medium zucchinis, trimmed and thinly sliced
- salt and freshly ground pepper
- 4 garlic cloves, minced
- 1 tablespoon chopped fresh basil *or* parsley
- ½ cup grated Parmesan cheese

Preheat oven to 350 degrees F. Lightly coat a 9 x 13-inch baking dish with olive oil.

Arrange half of the zucchini slices over the bottom of the pan. Cover with half the tomatoes, sprinkle with salt and pepper, and drizzle with oil. Repeat layers. Sprinkle with garlic, herbs, salt, pepper, Parmesan, and olive oil. Bake 1 hour 15 minutes. Serve hot or room temperature.

SERVES 6

The Tomato Business
The latest wrinkle in bringing tomatoes to market year-round is the development of the genetically engineered tomato by the Calgene Company of Davis, California. By altering the DNA of a tomato, they developed a tomato that ripens slowly, off the vine. The tomato stays firm and develops flavor as it is being shipped.

PICKLED TOMATOES

This wonderful, spicy pickling combination comes from Chefs Mary Sue Milliken and Susan Feniger of the Border Grill in Santa Monica, California.

1½ pounds firm, red tomatoes,
    cut in wedges
1 jalapeño chile, stemmed and sliced
    with seeds
¾ cup white vinegar
2 tablespoons sugar
1 tablespoon salt
⅓ cup olive oil
2 teaspoons minced fresh ginger
4 garlic cloves, minced
1 tablespoon mustard seeds
1 tablespoon cracked black peppercorns
½ teaspoon fennel seeds
1 teaspoon celery seeds

Combine tomatoes and jalapeño in large bowl.

Combine vinegar, sugar, and salt in saucepan. Bring to boil and cook, stirring occasionally, until liquid is clear. Set aside.

Heat olive oil in skillet over high heat. Cook ginger, garlic, mustard seed, peppercorns, and fennel, less than 1 minute, just to release aroma. Remove from heat and stir in vinegar mixture. Immediately pour over tomatoes. Mix well, cover with plastic wrap, and chill at least 3 days.

MAKES 3 CUPS

GRILLED TOMATOES WITH GARLIC MAYONNAISE

These warm tomatoes with mayonnaise are an excellent accompaniment for casual barbecues.

1/4 cup mayonnaise
3 garlic cloves, minced
1 tablespoon lemon juice
freshly ground pepper
2 large tomatoes, halved
olive oil for brushing
salt

Whisk together mayonnaise, garlic, lemon juice, and pepper. Set aside.

Preheat grill or broiler. Brush tomatoes with oil, sprinkle with salt, and grill cut-side to flame. Cover, if grilling, and cook until hot and juicy, about 4 minutes. Transfer to serving plate. Serve hot, topped with a dollop of garlic mayonnaise.

SERVES 4

A Fungus Among Us
The average American tomato consumer now consumes about 18 pounds a year of that "mere fungus of an offensive plant," as tomatoes were labeled by the editor of the Boston Courier *in the 1850s.*

ROASTED GARLIC TOMATOES

These caramelized tomato halves appear regularly at my house as an accompaniment to veal, lamb, chicken, or beef. Nothing could be easier.

4 medium tomatoes, halved
3 garlic cloves, minced
4 teaspoons olive oil
coarse salt

Preheat oven to 325 degrees F.

Arrange tomatoes, cut-side up, on foil-lined baking tray. Sprinkle with garlic, drizzle with olive oil, and season with salt. Bake until centers soften and skins begin to shrink, about 1½ hours. Serve warm or at room temperature.

SERVES 4

TOMATO
SCRAPS

TOMATO CONCASSE

A French concasse—a simple, uncooked, mild salsa of chopped tomatoes—is an easy way to dress up grilled chicken or fish.

3 medium tomatoes, chopped
2 tablespoons olive oil
1 teaspoon minced garlic
1 tablespoon chopped fresh basil
salt and freshly ground pepper

Combine all the ingredients in a small bowl and let sit at room temperature as long as 2 hours. Refrigerate up to 1 day.

MAKES 3 CUPS

TOMATO BUTTER

Spread this fragrant pink butter on toasted olive bread, steamed vegetables, or chicken and fish hot off the grill.

1 medium tomato, peeled, seeded, and chopped
¼ teaspoon minced garlic
salt
6 tablespoons butter, softened

Combine tomato, garlic, and pinch of salt in small saucepan. Bring to boil and reduce till nearly dry, about 5 minutes. Transfer to blender with butter. Pulse to combine and pour into small crock or mold. Refrigerate or freeze until solid.

MAKES ½ CUP

TOMATO GINGER CHUTNEY

This sharply flavored, chunky condiment adds an exotic note to turkey burgers, boiled shrimp, rice, or your favorite spicy sausage.

1/2 cup water
2 1/2 tablespoons sugar
2 teaspoons coarse salt
1/2 lemon, thinly sliced and halved,
    with seeds
2-inch length fresh ginger, peeled and very
    thinly sliced
2 teaspoons mild vegetable oil
1 cup diced red onion
3 medium tomatoes, peeled and chopped
freshly ground pepper
1 tablespoon cider vinegar

Combine water, 2 tablespoons of sugar, salt, lemon, and ginger in small saucepan. Bring to boil, reduce to simmer, and cook 10 minutes. Remove lemon and ginger slices and reserve along with $1/4$ cup cooking liquid.

Heat oil in a medium saucepan over moderate heat. Sauté onions until soft, about 3 minutes. Add tomatoes, lemon slices, ginger slices, reserved cooking liquid, pepper to taste, and remaining $1/2$ tablespoon sugar. Bring to boil, reduce to simmer, and cook about 15 minutes to thicken. Stir in vinegar, cook less than 1 minute, and remove from heat. Cool and store in refrigerator for up to 1 week or freeze.

MAKES 2 CUPS

HOMEMADE KETCHUP

*Until it got supplanted by salsa in the '90s,
ketchup was America's most popular condiment.
This upscale version was inspired by food editor
Bev Bennett of Chicago. Reserve for better than
french-fried occasions.*

2 teaspoons olive oil
2 shallots, minced
2 teaspoons grated fresh ginger
3 plum tomatoes, peeled, seeded,
    and diced
1 tablespoon cider vinegar
1 tablespoon honey
4 cloves
1/8 teaspoon cinnamon
3/4 teaspoon salt and freshly ground pepper

Heat oil in medium saucepan over medium-high heat. Sauté shallots and ginger until soft, about 4 minutes. Add remaining ingredients. Bring to a boil, reduce to a simmer, and cook, stirring frequently, until thickened, 20 minutes. Purée or crush with potato masher. Chill and serve.

MAKES ½ CUP, ENOUGH FOR 4 TOPPINGS

Tomato Condiment Mania

The New York Tribune *declared ketchup the national condiment back in 1896. Ever since, tomatoes, either preserved in the sweet-and-sour base known as ketchup, or mixed with onions and spices and bottled as salsa, have been adding zest to the American table in a major way.*

OVEN-DRIED TOMATOES

plum tomatoes
salt
olive oil

Halve tomatoes lengthwise and place on cake rack on baking sheet. Sprinkle with salt, and bake in 200 degrees F oven until dry and pliable, 8 to 10 hours. Turn once or twice during baking. Store in refrigerator, in sealed container, with oil to cover.

TOMATO-INFUSED OLIVE OIL

Here is a quick dressing for summertime pasta.

½ cup olive oil
3 garlic cloves, minced
3 plum tomatoes, seeded and diced
salt and freshly ground pepper

Combine oil and garlic in small saucepan. Cook over high heat until garlic is fragrant but not colored. Add tomatoes, salt, and pepper. Reduce heat to low, and cook until tomato liquid is released and boiled away, 8 to 10 minutes. Cool and store in sealed container in refrigerator.

MAKES ½ CUP

MEXICAN RED RICE

A fresh version of the standard Mexican restaurant accompaniment.

1 medium tomato, chopped
1/2 small onion, chopped
2 garlic cloves, peeled
2 tablespoons vegetable oil
1 cup long grain rice
1/2 teaspoon salt
1/4 teaspoon ground cumin
freshly ground pepper
1 1/2 cups chicken stock

Combine tomato, onion, and garlic in blender, and purée.

Heat oil in medium saucepan over medium-high heat. Add the rice, stirring frequently, until opaque and golden. Add the tomato purée, salt, cumin, and pepper, and cook, stirring frequently, until most of the liquid is absorbed. Pour in chicken stock, bring to a boil, reduce to a simmer, and cover. Cook 25 minutes, or until dry. Let sit with cover on about 10 minutes. Fluff with fork and serve.

SERVES 4

SUN-DRIED TOMATO PESTO

A great, lusty spread for grilled bread or a bowl of pasta. Strong cheeses like goat or feta are a natural complement of sun-dried tomatoes.

1/2 cup sun-dried tomatoes packed in oil, chopped
1/4 cup Kalamata olives, sliced off pit
2 tablespoons pine nuts
1 teaspoon minced garlic
2 teaspoons fresh thyme leaves
2 tablespoons dry white wine *or* lemon juice
1/2 cup olive oil

Combine tomatoes, olives, pine nuts, garlic, thyme, and wine in blender and purée to a paste. With machine on, drizzle in olive oil and purée. Serve on pasta or use as a spread.

MAKES ¾ CUP, ENOUGH FOR 1 POUND PASTA

SWEET SURPRISES AND MORE

THE BLOODY MARY

The classic American cure for a hangover. Add spice to taste.

ice cubes
1 (1½-ounce) shot vodka
1 cup tomato juice
⅛ teaspoon salt
Worcestershire sauce
Tabasco sauce
freshly ground black pepper
lime wedge *or* small celery rib with leaves
    attached, for garnish

Fill a tall glass with ice. Pour in the vodka, tomato juice, salt, a couple of dashes Worcestershire, and Tabasco sauce to taste. Stir. Sprinkle top with fresh pepper and garnish with lime wedge or celery rib.
SERVES 1

TOMATO LIME ICE

This rustic Italian ice—or granita—can be made by hand, without any special equipment. Serve after an Italian-style summer barbecue.

> 2 medium tomatoes, peeled, seeded, and diced
> 1½ cups water
> ½ cup sugar
> 1 teaspoon salt
> 3 sprigs thyme
> ¼ cup lime juice

Purée tomatoes in blender to make about 1 cup pulp.

Combine water, sugar, salt, and thyme in heavy saucepan. Bring to a boil and cook, stirring occasionally, until clear syrup is formed, about 2 minutes. Remove from heat and discard thyme. Stir in tomato purée and lime juice. Pour into round metal cake pan and freeze about 45 minutes. Then remove and with a spoon, stir and break up ice crystals. Return to freezer and stir every 15 minutes until a granular slush forms. Serve in glass cups or store in plastic container in freezer.

SERVES 4 TO 6

Tomatoes in Space
After the U.S. space program sent millions of tomato seeds into space as a science experiment back in 1984, NASA brought them back and asked science teachers to grow them in the classroom—with one caveat: Students were instructed not to eat the potentially mutant space tomatoes.

SUN-DRIED TOMATO ANISETTE BISCOTTI

A savory biscuit for afternoon espresso.

1 stick butter, softened
1/4 cup sugar
2 eggs
2 teaspoons Pernod *or* Sambuca
2 cups plus 2 tablespoons flour
1 1/2 teaspoons baking powder
1/2 teaspoon salt
2 tablespoons anise *or* fennel seeds
2 tablespoons drained, rinsed, and
   chopped oil-packed sun-dried tomatoes

Preheat oven to 350 degrees F.

Cream together butter and sugar until smooth. Beat in the eggs and then Pernod.

In another bowl, stir together flour, baking powder, salt, and anise or fennel seeds. Add to the butter mixture and stir just until combined. Lightly beat in tomatoes.

Transfer to lightly floured board and knead into smooth ball. Cut in half. Pat and roll each half into 10 x 3-inch logs. Place on uncoated baking sheets and bake until dry, about 35 minutes.

Remove, leaving oven on, and cool slightly. Transfer to cutting board and cut each loaf into $\frac{1}{2}$-inch slices. Return to tray, cut-side up, and bake 10 minutes longer per side. Let cool and store in cookie jar or tin.

MAKES 24 BISCUITS

CONVERSIONS

LIQUID
1 Tbsp = 15 ml
½ cup = 4 fl oz = 125 ml
1 cup = 8 fl oz = 250 ml

DRY
¼ cup = 4 Tbsp = 2 oz = 60 g
1 cup = ½ pound = 8 oz = 250 g

FLOUR
½ cup = 60 g
1 cup = 4 oz = 125 g

TEMPERATURE
400° F = 200° C = gas mark 6
375° F = 190° C = gas mark 5
350° F = 175° C = gas mark 4

MISCELLANEOUS
2 Tbsp butter = 1 oz = 30 g
1 inch = 2.5 cm
all-purpose flour = plain flour
baking soda = bicarbonate of soda
brown sugar = demerara sugar
confectioners' sugar = icing sugar
heavy cream = double cream
molasses = black treacle
raisins = sultanas
rolled oats = oat flakes
semisweet chocolate = plain chocolate
sugar = caster sugar